- For my son, Marek
who calls this prayer "The Bread Prayer"

Thank you to Mrs. Ludeman  for teaching him
"Give us today our daily bread."

# Birch Blossom
## Books

## Watertown, WI

# Baby's First Lord's Prayer

## A Lutheran High Contrast Book

*By Keely Marie Prekop*

Our Father in heaven, hallowed be your name,

Your kingdom come, Your will be done,

On earth as in heaven.

Give us today our daily bread.

Forgive us
our sins,

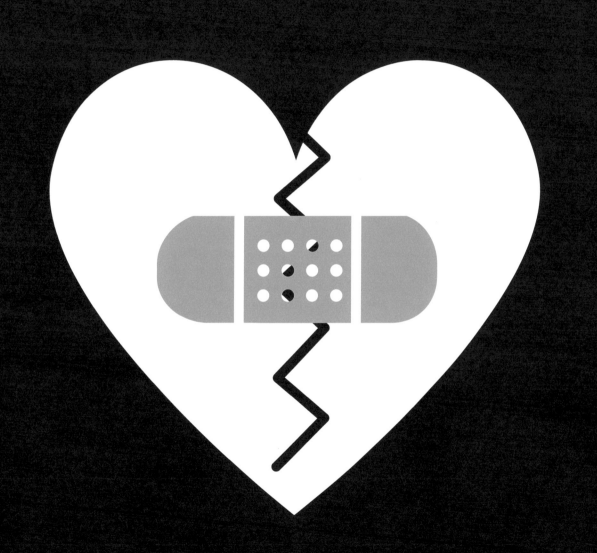

As we forgive those who sin against us.

Lead us not into temptation,

# But deliver us from evil.

For the kingdom, the power, and the glory

Are yours now
and forever.

Amen.

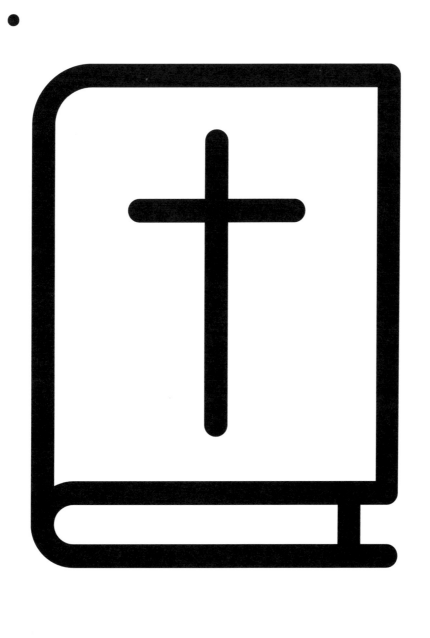

# My Top 5 Reasons for
# Why I Teach My Children to Pray

**1) Who do I want my children to turn to with their struggles? God or the world?** In today's age, what do you if you don't know something? You Google it! We live in an age of people who are constantly over and under informed. Anyone can give answers to everyone's problems 24/7. But who vets these answers? I want my children to go to their all-knowing Lord, not some online consensus forum where anyone can tell them to do things that might end up hurting them. (Romans 12:12, 1 Peter 5:7)

**2) The best way to learn something is to teach someone else.** This may be my teacher background speaking, but the most confident I ever feel about a topic is after I have prepared myself to teach someone else about it. You anticipate questions, you think through reasons of traditions, and question practices you may have never questioned before. It gives you a deeper appreciation for why you do the things you do. This is true for teaching your child about God, church, or even praying. (Deuteronomy 6:6,7, Matthew 6:9)

**3) Prayer gives my children a direct line of communication to their Creator and Savior.** What other all-knowing, all-powerful being would be willing to listen to my son discuss his favorite airplanes and ask for the ability to fly one someday? I gave birth to them and still don't always have the patience to listen to my children's ramblings. However, our LORD loves hearing from them. This allows my child build a relationship before a crisis arrives. This way, when a crisis arrives in their life, they won't hesitate to go to the most powerful being who cares about them on a level that no one else does, (2 Chronicles 20:6, Romans 3:12)

**4) As I teach my children to thank God for their blessings, their gratitude is given the chance to increase.** This one is true for myself too. While living life, I can get bogged down and impatient with the blessings and the timing of those blessings that God gives me. My children can be the same way. However, during daily prayers, if you are able to set aside time to thank God for at least three things each day, it opens your child's and your eyes to all the blessings God has already surrounded you with. (1 Thessalonians 5:16-18)

**5) I want my children to develop a deep, active, and authentic relationship with God.** Just memorizing Bible passages and prayers is not enough to meet the end goal of Christian parenting. I want my children to understand the words they are saying. I want them to know that they can and should talk to God about anything and everything. My son should be just as comfortable talking to God about being scared of the dark, being nervous about going to new places, and missing loved ones who have passed, just as easily as telling God about his dinosaurs, cars, and airplanes. (Matthew 19:14)

God has blessed us with these tiny humans. It's amazing how God formed them, planned for them, and entrusted them to us. We can understand the importance of the responsibility given to us but we can also trust in God's promises that he is watching over them and has plans to prosper them. cannot wait to watch them and their faith grow,

Made in United States
Troutdale, OR
12/28/2023

16514131R00017